All copyrighted content reprinted by permission of the copyright owners.
No part of this course reader may be reproduced, in any form without permission of the rights holders.

Copyright © 2011 by Princeton University Press

Published by Princeton University Press
41 William Street, Princeton, New Jersey 08540

In the United Kingdom: Princeton University Press
6 Oxford Street, Woodstock, Oxfordshire OX20 1 TW

press.princeton.edu

All Rights Reserved

Library of Congress Control Number: 2011925431

ISBN 978-0-691-14836-6

British Library Cataloging-in-Publication Data is available

This book has been composed in STKaiti, Simsun, and Times New Roman

The publisher would like to acknowledge the authors of this volume for
providing the camera-ready copy from which this book was printed.

Printed on acid-free paper. ∞

Printed in the United States of America

7   9   10   8

新的中国
A New China

目 录
Table of Contents

第一课　到了北京

　　飞机是今天晚上七点钟准时降落在⑴北京首都国际机场的。学校外事处派来的一位张先生在机场接我们。

　　通过海关的时候儿，我有点儿⑵担心，因为我带了

北京	Běijīng	*n.*	Beijing
飞机	fēijī	*n.*	airplane
准时	zhǔnshí	*adv./adj.*	punctually; on time 准时上课/准时到学校来/他总是很 准时。
降落	jiàngluò	*v.*	land; descend
首都	shǒudū	*n.*	capital
国际	guójì	*adj.*	international
机场	jīchǎng	*n.*	airport
外事处	wàishìchù	*n.*	foreign affairs office
派	pài	*v.*	dispatch; send
张	Zhāng	*n.*	Zhang (a surname)
先生	xiān.sheng	*n.*	Mr.
接	jiē	*v.*	meet; welcome; fetch
通过	tōngguò	*v.*	pass; pass through; go through
海关	hǎiguān	*n.*	customs
担心	dānxīn	*v.*	worry; feel anxious 很担心/别担心 我很担心飞机不能准时降落。
带	dài	*v.*	take; bring; carry

几本儿《花花公子》给我的中国朋友。据说(3)中国海关对(4)这类杂志查得很严，好在(5)他们根本(6)没打开我的行李就让(7)我通过了。后来(8)我们坐上了一部大巴，开了差不多一个小时就到学校了。

花花公子	Huāhuā gōngzǐ	*n.*	*Playboy*
据说	jùshuō	*adv.*	it is said; they say
对	duì	*prep.*	about; toward; on; to
类	lèi	*n.*	type; category
杂志	zázhì	*n.*	magazine
查	chá	*v.*	check; inspect
严	yán	*adj.*	strict; severe; stern 老师很严。/学校对学生很严。
好在	hǎozài	*adv.*	luckily; fortunately
根本	gēnběn	*adv.*	utterly; completely; at all (always used in negative sentences) 根本没去/根本不会/根本听不懂
打开	dǎ//kāi	*v.-c.*	open
行李	xíng.li	*n.*	luggage; baggage
让	ràng	*v.*	let; allow
后来	hòulái	*n.*	afterwards
坐上	zuò//.shàng	*v.-c.*	get on (a vehicle)
部	bù	*AN*	measure word for cars or movies 一部汽车/一部电影
大巴	dàbā	*n.*	large bus
开（车）	kāi	*v.*	drive (a car)
差不多	chà .bu duō	*adv.*	around; about (a certain number) 睡了差不多十个小时 花了差不多一千块钱

北京给我的第一个印象(9)是海关的检查很松，没有我想的那么严。从机场到城里的高速公路又宽又(10)平，非常现代化。这和我想象中(11)古老的北京完全不同(12)。

今天很累，可是也很兴奋。我们的宿舍很好，房间很大，床也很舒服，不过因为时差的关系(13)，一直到早上三点还没睡着。

印象	yìnxiàng	n.	impression
检查	jiǎnchá	v./n.	check; examine; inspect; inspection
松	sōng	adj.	loose; slack
城里	chénglǐ	p.w.	within the city; downtown
高速公路	gāosù gōnglù	n.	expressway; freeway
宽	kuān	adj.	wide; broad
平	píng	adj.	flat; smooth; level
现代化	xiàndàihuà	adj./n.	modern, modernization
想象	xiǎngxiàng	v./n.	imagine, imagination
古老	gǔlǎo	adj.	ancient; age-old
兴奋	xīngfèn	adj.	excited
宿舍	sùshè	n.	dormitory
舒服	shū.fu	adj.	comfortable
不过	búguò	adv.	but; however
时差	shíchā	n.	jet lag; time difference
关系	guān.xi	n.	relevance, relationships (used with 因为 to indicate cause or reason)
一直	yìzhí	adv.	all the way; all along; continuously 我等他一直等到十点钟。
睡着	shuì//zháo	v.-c.	fall asleep

★ **繁体字课文** (fǎntǐzì kèwén, **Text in Traditional Characters**)

　　飛機是今天晚上七點鐘準時降落在⑴北京首都國際機場的。學校外事處派來的一位張先生在機場接我們。

　　通過海關的時候儿，我有點儿⑵擔心，因為我帶了幾本儿《花花公子》給我的中國朋友。據說⑶中國海關對⑷這類雜誌查得很嚴，好在⑸他們根本⑹沒打開我的行李就讓⑺我通過了。後來⑻我們坐上了一部大巴，開了差不多一個小時就到學校了。

　　北京給我的第一個印象⑼是海關的檢查很鬆，沒有我想的那麼嚴。從機場到城裏的高速公路又寬又⑽平，非常現代化。這和我想像中⑾古老的北京完全不同⑿。

　　今天很累，可是也很興奮。我們的宿舍很好，房間很大，床也很舒服，不過因為時差的關係⒀，一直到早上三點還沒睡着。

〰 **语法点** (yǔfǎdiǎn, **Grammar Notes**)

⑴ 飞机是今天晚上七点钟准时降落**在**北京首都国际机场的。

It was at seven o'clock this evening that the plane landed as scheduled at Beijing Capital International Airport.

Together with a word or phrase denoting place, 在 forms a prepositional phrase which can be placed before a verb as an adverbial phrase. For instance, in 在图书馆看书 or 在饭馆里吃饭, the 在 construction indicates the place where an action occurs. When placed after the verb as a complement, the 在 phrase can also indicate the place at which a person or thing has arrived after or as a result of the action, e.g. 放在桌子上, or 降落在国际机场. Moreover, verbs such as 住 and 降落

can be modified by either the 在 adverbial or the 在 complement; therefore, it is possible to say 降落在国际机场 or 在国际机场降落.

(2) 通过海关的时候儿，我**有点儿**担心。

When I passed through customs, I was a little worried.

有一点儿+ *adj.* indicates a small degree of something dissatisfactory or disagreeable. It can modify negative adjective forms. The "一" can also optionally be dropped.

1. 昨天我有一点儿不舒服。

I felt a little uncomfortable yesterday.

2. 我今天有点儿累。

I am a bit tired today.

(3) **据说**中国海关对这类杂志查得很严。

It is said that China's customs is very strict about inspecting this kind of magazine.

据说 introduces hearsay. The phrase may sometimes be split to provide additional information. Note: This phrase is in the passive voice, and thus a subject like "我" or "你" cannot be added before it.

1. 据说他来中国以前，只学了一年中文。

It is said that he studied only one year of Chinese before he came to China.

2. 据学校派来的张先生说，现在的北京和从前完全不同了。

According to Mr. Zhang, the man whom the school sent, present-day Beijing is completely different from the old Beijing.

(4) 据说中国海关**对**这类杂志查得很严。

对 often takes a noun or verb-object construction as its object, which is the recipient of the verb that follows.

1. 他对中国的情况知道得很少。

He knows very little about China's situation.

2. 我对北京的机场有很好的印象。

I have a very good impression of Beijing's airport.

(5) **好在**他们根本没打开我的行李就让我通过了。

Fortunately, they let me pass without opening my luggage at all.

好在 points out an advantageous condition in unfavorable circumstances. It is an adverb, and there is no negative form.

1. 这是我第一次到北京来，我有点儿紧张。好在学校派来的张先生在机场接我。

This was the first that I'd been to Beijing, and I was a little nervous. Fortunately, Mr. Zhang, the man whom the school sent, was at the airport to meet me.

2. 好在学校不太远，开车差不多一个钟头就能到。

Luckily the school is not too far. You can get there in about one hour by driving.

(6) 好在他们**根本**没打开我的行李就让我通过了。

根本 usually modifies a negative form and conveys a strong feeling.

1. 海关的检查根本不严，你不必担心。

The customs inspection isn't strict at all. You don't need to worry.

2. 他根本不会开车，你怎么能让他去机场接人呢？

He doesn't know how to drive at all. How could you ask him to pick someone up at the airport?

(7) 好在他们根本没打开我的行李就**让**我通过了。

让 in this context means "to let" or "to allow (someone to do something)."

1. 这件事让他做吧！

Let him do it.

2. 我妈妈不让我一边吃东西一边看书。

My mother doesn't allow me to eat and read at the same time.

(8) **后来**我们坐上了一部大巴。

Later on we rode in a large bus.

后来 and 然后 both mean afterwards, but 后来 can be used only to describe events which have already transpired. 然后 indicates the sequence of what's happening. The pattern is often 先⋯，然后（再，又，还）⋯.

1. A: 后来怎么样？ B: 后来海关就让我通过了。

   A: What happened afterwards?   B: Afterwards, customs let me
                                              passed.

2. 我想先去北京，然后去别的地方。

   I plan to go to Beijing first and go to other places afterwards.

3. 他先买了一本书，然后又买了几只笔。

   He bought a book and then bought a few pens as well.

(9) 北京**给我**的第一个**印象**是海关的检查很松。

The first impression that Beijing gave me is that the customs is lax.

    北京给我的第一个印象 means "the first impression that Beijing gave me." This idea can also be expressed as "我对北京的第一个印象."

1. 北京首都国际机场给我们的印象很好。

   The Beijing Capital International Airport impressed us very much.

2. 高速公路又宽又平，给了我们很好的印象。

   We were impressed by how wide and level the highway was.

3. 我对那个学生的印象是：他很爱说话。

   The impression I have of that student is that he is quite talkative.

4. 我对中国海关的印象很好。

   My impression of China's customs is very favorable.

(10) 从机场到城里的高速公路**又宽又平**。

The highway from the airport to the city is both wide and flat.

    With verbs, adjectives, or phrases, the pattern 又⋯又⋯ indicates that two or more actions, states, or qualities coexist.

1. 我们的宿舍又大又舒服。

   Our dorm is both big and comfortable.

2. 他又会说中文又会说英文。

   He can speak Chinese, and he can speak English.

3. 昨天晚上他们又吃又喝，花了不少钱。

They ate and drank last night, spending more than a little money.

(11) 这和我想象**中**古老的北京完全不同。

This Beijing and the ancient one I had imagined are completely different.

中 means "middle;" therefore, 想象中 means "in one's imagination," 生活中的困难 means "the problems in one's life" and 社会中的问题 means "the issues in a society." The structure "verb 中" also means "in the middle of verb."

(12) 这**和**我想象中古老的北京完全**不同**。

A 和 B 不同 means A is different from B. Do not use 同 for positive forms; instead use 一样.

1. 这本杂志和我想象中的有点儿不同。
   This magazine is a little different from what I imagined.

2. 北京的海关和美国的一样，都检查得很松。
   Beijing customs is just like customs in America, it is very lax.

(13) **因为**时差**的关系**，一直到早上三点还没睡着。

Because of jet lag, I did not fall asleep until after three o'clock in the morning.

关系 means "relations," "influence" or "relevance." When it is used with 因为, it indicates cause or reason. The expression 因为...的关系 may be used with a reason which is slightly vague.

1. 因为天气的关系，飞机不能准时降落。
   Because of the weather, the airplane was unable to land on schedule.

2. 因为时间的关系，我们就谈到这儿。
   We will have to stop because of the time.

✏ 练习（liànxí, Exercise）

I. Answer the following questions using the structures provided.

1. 你为什么要学中文呢？（因为…的关系）

2. 你来中国以前，对中国有什么样的印象？（据说）

3. 你来中国，坐飞机坐了多长时间？（V. 了+time duration 的 O.）

4. 你对北京首都国际机场的第一个印象是什么？（又…又…）

5. 你到中国以前，最担心什么？现在还担心吗？（好在）

6. 中国的海关严还是美国的海关严？（A 没有 B 那么 adj.）

II. Choose the correct answer in parentheses to complete each sentence.

1. 他现在又高又黑，和我想象（上，中，下）完全不同。

2. （我据说，据中国海关说）《花花公子》不能带进中国。

3. 我们应该先到宿舍去，（后来，然后）到外事处去。

4. 要通过海关的人不多，我们花了半个小时（就，不过，还）通过检查了。

5. 走高速公路很快，（从机场到学校，开从机场到学校）只要一个小时。

6. 他一（坐了上，坐上了）车就（睡不着，不睡着）。

7. 我们对学生（一点儿，有一点儿）松，我（担心一点儿，有一点儿担心）。

III. Make a sentence using the underlined structure(s).

1. 通过海关的<u>时候儿</u>，我<u>有点儿</u>担心，<u>因为</u>我带了几本儿《花花公子》给我的中国朋友。

2. <u>据说</u>中国海关对这类杂志查得很严，好在他们没打开行李就让我通过了。

3. 今天很累，也很兴奋。不过<u>因为</u>时差<u>的关系</u>，一直到早上三点还没睡着。

IV. Combine the following pairs of sentences into a single sentence.

Example: 张先生在学校的外事处工作。他到机场来接我。

→ 在学校外事处工作的张先生到机场来接我。

1. 我跟一个美国学生住在一起。他只学了一个月中文。

2. 我的中国朋友到宿舍来看我。他们住在北京。

3. 中国的海关打开了行李。行李里有《花花公子》杂志。

4. 外事处派来一部大巴。我们坐上了大巴。

V. Complete the dialogues with the expressions provided.

1. A: 你学中文已经两年了，你不想到中国看看吗？

 B: ＿＿＿＿＿＿＿＿＿＿。（因为…的关系，一直还…）

2. A: 你对这个学校宿舍的印象怎么样？

 B: 不太好，＿＿＿＿＿＿＿＿。（又…又…，有点儿adj.）

3. A: 通过海关的时候，你担心吗？

 B: ＿＿＿＿＿＿＿＿＿＿。（一点儿也不，因为，根本）

VI. Translate into Chinese.

1. Don't worry! There are not many cars on the highway from downtown to the airport at this time (of day). You will be able to catch (use "坐上") the airplane on time.

2. This school is not as modernized as I thought. The dormitory is old and small. It is totally different from what I had imagined.

3. Because of 911, Customs at American airports is very strict. If you have water in your luggage, they simply won't let you pass.

4. I waited at the airport until 6 o'clock, but didn't see Mr. Zhang, dispatched from the foreign affairs office.

VII. Composition

Write a journal of what you see in your first day/week here in China. What is your first impression? What surprises you most? Have you seen any stark contrasts: new and old, fast and slow, modern and traditional? As a new visitor, what do you think about these extremes?

第二课　给妈妈打电话

女：妈，我已经到了北京了，一切都很顺利。

母：那(1)我就放心了。你累不累啊？

女：累是有点儿累(2)，可是很兴奋。

母：宿舍怎么样啊？是单人间还是双人间？

女：是双人间。同屋是个美国学生，我们很谈得来(3)。

电话	diànhuà	n.	telephone; phone call
打电话	dǎ diànhuà	v.-o.	make a phone call; call
			给他打了一个电话
			打了一个电话给他
一切	yíqiè	n.	all; every; everything (一切 is usually followed by 都.)
顺利	shùnlì	adj.	smooth; successful
放心	fàng//xīn	v.-o.	set one's mind at rest; feel relieved
单人间	dānrénjiān	n.	single room
双人间	shuāngrénjiān	n.	double room
同屋	tóngwū	n.	roommate
谈得来	tán .de lái	v.-c.	get along well (negative form: 谈不来)
			我跟他很谈得来。

母：那很好。天气预报说今年夏天北京特别热，宿舍

里有空调吗？

女：有。不但⑷有空调，还有电视、电话、热水和自己

的浴室呢！

母：这样的条件比⑸你在美国的宿舍还好嘛⑹！

女：是啊！每天还有人给我们换毛巾、整理床铺、打

扫房间呢！

天气	tiānqì	n.	weather
预报	yùbào	n.	forecast
夏天	xiàtiān	n.	summer
特别	tèbié	adv./adj.	especially, special
			特别快/特别有意思/很特别
热	rè	adj.	hot
空调	kōngtiáo	n.	air-conditioning
电视	diànshì	n.	television
浴室	yùshì	n.	bathroom; washroom
条件	tiáojiàn	n.	condition
			宿舍的条件非常好。
嘛	.ma		modal particle
换	huàn	v.	change
			换衣服/换钱
毛巾	máojīn	n.	towel
整理	zhěnglǐ	v.	put in order; straighten up
			整理房间
床铺	chuángpù	n.	bedding
打扫	dǎsǎo	v.	sweep; clean

母：这听起来(7)简直(8)像个旅馆。学校太照顾外国学生

了。我真(9)担心你们要被(10)惯坏了。

女：住得舒服点儿才(11)能好好儿学习啊！

母：校园怎么样呢？安全不安全啊？

女：听说(12)安全得很，而且校园里又有饭馆儿又有商店，

留学生食堂离(13)我的宿舍也很近，方便极了。

简直	jiǎnzhí	adv.	simply; virtually	简直太好了
旅馆	lǚguǎn	n.	hotel	
照顾	zhào.gù	v.	take care of; look after	
惯坏	guàn//huài	v.-c.	spoil 把孩子惯坏了	
学习	xuéxí	v.	study	
校园	xiàoyuán	n.	campus	
安全	ānquán	adj.	safe	
听说	tīngshuō	v.	be told; hear of; hear 听说海关检查得很严。	
adj.得很	....dehěn		very 好得很/方便得很	
而且	érqiě	conj.	and; as well (as), furthermore	
饭馆儿	fànguǎnr	n.	restaurant	
商店	shāngdiàn	n.	store; shop	
留学生	liúxuéshēng	n.	foreign student	
食堂	shítáng	n.	dining hall	
离	lí	v.	be away from; from	
近	jìn	adj.	close; near	

母：去了北京，条件又⑭那么好，要是再⑮学不好中

文，可⑯就没有借口了。

女：您放心，我会努力学习的。

母：你一方面⑰要努力学习，一方面也得注意健康啊！

女：我知道。妈，国际长途电话太贵了，下星期再给

您打吧！再见再见！

母：好，好。再见再见！

方便	fāngbiàn	*adj.*	convenient
adj. 极了	...jíle		extremely; very 好极了/舒服极了/担心极了
借口	jièkǒu	*n.*	excuse
您	nín	*pron.*	you (polite form)
努力	nǔlì	*adv./adj.*	with great effort 特别努力/努力工作
方面	fāngmiàn	*n.*	respect; aspect; side
得	děi	*v.*	must; have to
注意	zhùyì	*v.*	pay attention to 注意听/没注意这件事
健康	jiànkāng	*n./adj.*	health; physique, healthy
长途	chángtú	*adj.*	long distance 长途电话/长途车

★ **繁体字课文**（fántǐzì kèwén, Text in Traditional Characters）

女：媽，我已經到了北京了，一切都很順利。

母：那⑴我就放心了。你累不累啊？

女：累是有點兒累⑵，可是很興奮。

母：宿舍怎麼樣啊？是單人間還是雙人間？

女：是雙人間。同屋是個美國學生，我們很談得來⑶。

母：那很好。天氣預報說今年夏天北京特別熱，宿舍裏有空調嗎？

女：有。不但⑷有空調，還有電視、電話、熱水和自己的浴室呢！

母：這樣的條件比⑸你在美國的宿舍還好嘛⑹！

女：是啊！每天還有人給我們換毛巾、整理床鋪、打掃房間呢！

母：這聽起來⑺簡直⑻像個旅館。學校太照顧外國學生了。我真⑼擔心你們要被⑽慣壞了。

女：住得舒服點兒才⑾能好好兒學習啊！

母：校園怎麼樣呢？安全不安全啊？

女：聽說⑿安全得很，而且校園裏又有飯館兒又有商店，留學生食堂離⒀我的宿舍也很近，方便極了。

母：去了北京，條件又⒁那麼好，要是再⒂學不好中文，可⒃就沒有藉口了。

女：您放心，我會努力學習的。

母：你一方面⒄要努力學習，一方面也得注意健康啊！

女：我知道。媽，國際長途電話太貴了，下星期再給您打吧！再見再見！

母：好，好。再見再見！

✎ 语法点 （yǔfǎdiǎn, Grammar Notes）

(1) **那**我就放心了。

Then I won't worry about it.

那 here means " in that case" or "then."

1. 要是你不累，**那**我们就开始打扫房间吧！
   If you're not tired, then let's start to clean the room.

2. 房间里有电话，**那**你就可以常给父母打电话了。
   There is a phone in your room; you may call your parents often then.

(2) 累**是**有点儿累，**可是**很兴奋。

I was a bit tired, but I was very excited.

是 can be inserted between verbs or adjectives to make a concession, usually followed by 但是，不过，可是, etc. Adverbs can modify the repeated verb or adjectives, but must be placed immediately before the second occurrence or before both occurrences.

1. 海关的检查严**是**不严，但是你最好别带不该带的东西。
   You are right, the customs inspection is not strict, but you'd better not bring anything that you shouldn't be bringing.

2. 他的行李大**是**大，不过并不重。
   His baggage may be large, but it is not heavy.

(3) 我们很**谈得来**。

We get along well.

谈得来 means "get along well." The negative form is 谈不来. Use 跟 to introduce the object.

1. 我跟他虽然是新朋友，可是很谈得来。
   Although he and I are only new friends, we get along very well.

2. 你跟你的同屋谈不来啊？那真糟糕！
   You don't get along well with your roommate? That's really too bad!

(4) **不但**有空调，**还**有电视、电话和自己的浴室呢！

We not only have air-conditioning, but also a color TV, a telephone and a private bathroom.

不但 is used in the first clause of a complex sentence in conjunction with 而且, 并且, 也 or 还 in the second clause to introduce a further statement which expands upon the initial one.

1. 这个校园不但漂亮而且安全。

This campus is not only pretty, but also safe.

2. 你不但得努力学习，也得注意健康。

Not only must you study hard, you must also pay attention to your health.

(5) 这样的条件**比**你在美国的宿舍**还**好嘛！．

These kinds of conditions are even better than your dorm in America.

"A 比 B 还 *adj.*" means "A is even more *adj.* than B." When 还 is stressed, it indicates that the situation is surprising or unexpected.

1. 北京虽然是个古老的城市，可是高速公路比美国的还好。

Beijing may be an old city, but the highways there are even better than those in the States.

2. 我们的房间比旅馆的还舒服。

Our rooms are even more comfortable than those in a hotel.

3. 没想到北京的夏天比美国的还热！

I never thought that the summer in Beijing could be even hotter than summer in America!

(6) 这样的条件比你在美国的宿舍还好**嘛**！

When 嘛 occurs at the end of a declarative sentence, it emphasizes affirmation and shows that a reason or cause is obvious.

1. 又有空调，又有电视和电话，这个房间很不错嘛！

This room has air-conditioning, a color TV and a telephone; it is not bad at all!

2. 他说得比我好，因为他学的时间比我长嘛！

Of course he speaks better than I do -- because he has studied longer than I have!

(7) 这听**起来**简直像个旅馆。

This place sounds just like a hotel.

When 起来 follows the verbs such as 看, 听, 闻 or 吃, it means "it appears," "it sounds," "it smells," and "it tastes" respectively.

1. 听起来这个学校很照顾外国学生。
   It sounds like the school takes good care of foreign students.

2. 这个菜看起来不错，不知道吃起来怎么样。
   This dish looks good; I wonder how it tastes.

(8) 这听起来**简直**像个旅馆。

简直 is an emphatic expression meaning "simply, at all," and usually modifies descriptive words and phrases, which may imply exaggeration or emphasis.

1. 这本杂志简直太有意思了！
   This magazine is so interesting!

2. 这个宿舍的条件简直太好了！
   The conditions in this dormitory are simply terrific!

3. 他简直一个朋友都没有！
   He simply has no friends at all!

(9) 我**真**担心你们要被惯坏了。
    I am really worried that you will be spoiled.

真 means "really," "truly," or "indeed." It is used to indicate the truth of a fact and also for emphasis.

1. 这个校园真好，又大又漂亮。
   This campus is really great! It is big and pretty.

2. 每天都有人给我们换毛巾，整理床铺，学校真太照顾外国学生了。
   There is somebody who comes to change our towels and make our beds everyday. The school really takes good care of foreign students.

真 is used in exclamatory sentences only. To say "This is a very good university," use the expression 这是一个很好的大学 instead of 这是一个真好的大学。For more information about this usage, see L. 46, Note (4).

(10) 我真担心你们要**被**惯坏了。

被 is a passive voice marker. The passive voice is usually expressed in the following pattern: receiver of action + 被 + doer of action + other elements, e.g. 这个孩子被父母惯坏了.

When the doer needs not or cannot be mentioned, 被 can be placed immediately before the verb. All adverbs, including 不 and 没, come before 被, not immediately before the verb. In general, verbs used with 被 are transitive and must take some post-element to explain how they affect their subjects. Originally, the 被 pattern applied to events concerning human beings, and verbs used were inflictive in most cases. Under the influence of western languages, 被 now applies also to non-human events in science and in literature, and verbs may need not be inflictive, although they generally have negative connotations.

1. 所有的菜都被他一个人吃光了。

   He ate all the food. (All the food was eaten up by him.)

2. 我的车被我同屋开出去了。

   My roommate took my car. (My car was taken away by my roommate)

(11) 住得舒服点儿**才**能好好儿学习啊!

Only by living a little more comfortably can one study well.

才 in the second clause indicates that the first clause is the necessary condition, without which the result in the second clause would be impossible.

1. 房间里一定得有空调才能住得舒服。

   A room must have air-conditioning for one to be able to live there comfortably.

2. 天天说中文才能说得很好。

   Only by speaking Chinese everyday can one speak Chinese well.

(12) **听说**校园安全得很。

I heard that the campus is very safe.

听说 differs from 据说 in that 听说 can take a subject and can be modified by 没 or 从来没...过.

1. 听说留学生宿舍的条件特别好。

   They say that the living conditions in the foreign students' dormitories are especially good.

2. 我听说他跟同屋谈不来，是真的吗？

I heard that he doesn't get along with his roommate. Is that true?

3. 我从来没听说过这件事。

I have never heard of this before.

(13) 留学生食堂**离**我的宿舍也很近。

The foreign students' dining hall is very close to my dorm.

离 is used to denote separation and to indicate distance.

1. 学校离机场很远，得开一个小时车才能到。

The school is quite far from the airport; it takes one hour of driving to get there.

2. 外事处离这儿并不远。

The Foreign Affairs Office is not far from here.

(14) 去了北京，条件**又**那么好，要是再学不好中文，可就没有借口了。

You are in Beijing, and your living conditions are so good; therefore, you have no excuse if you still cannot learn Chinese well.

又 means "on top of," "in addition to," or "moreover."

1. 我很兴奋，又有时差，所以睡不着觉。

In addition to having jet lag, I was also very excited, therefore I couldn't fall asleep.

2. 天气特别热，又没有空调，人人都觉得很不舒服。

It is very hot and there is no air-conditioning; everybody feels uncomfortable.

(15) 去了北京，条件又那么好，要是**再**学不好中文，可就没有借口了。

再 here indicates the continuation of an action which has not yet occurred or may possibly occur.

1. 不要再吃了！你吃得太多了！

Don't eat any more! You've eaten too much!

2. 要是你再这么说，我就要生气了。

If you keep talking like this, I will be angry.

⒃ 去了北京，条件又那么好，要是再学不好中文，**可**就没有借口了。

可 is used as an emphatic word meaning "surely," "certainly," or "finally." It is often followed by particles such as 了, 呀 or 啦 to make the sentence an exclamation.

1. 这本书我找了两个月，今天可买着了。
   I've been looking for this book for two months. I finally bought it today.

2. 你走了以后，可别忘了给我写信啊！
   Don't forget to write me after you leave.

⒄ 你**一方面**要努力学习，**一方面**也得注意健康啊！
On the one hand, you need to study hard, while on the other hand, you have to pay attention to your health.

With two words, phrases, or clauses, 一方面...一方面 indicates that two actions or situations coexist and may contrast with or supplement each other. 另 may occur before the second 一方面, and is often followed by 又, 也 or 还.

1. 我一方面想学中文，(另)一方面也想看看北京。
   I want to study Chinese and also want to see Beijing.

2. 我一方面想到外国去念书，可是(另)一方面又不愿意离开家。
   On the one hand, I want to study abroad, but on the other hand, I don't want to be away from home.

3. 一方面这家旅馆离车站太远，(另)一方面价钱也很贵，所以我们想换一个旅馆。
   We are thinking of switching to another hotel because this one is too far from the station and is also very expensive.

✎ 练习（liànxí, Exercise）

I. Answer the following questions using the expressions provided.

1. 要是没有人到机场接你，你怎么办？ （那 then）

2. 校园附近的饭馆都好不好？ （*adj.* 是 *adj.*，可是…）

3. 你喜欢这儿的宿舍吗？为什么？ （简直）

4. 你睡觉的时候，为什么一定要开空调？ （才）

5. 他的中文为什么说得这么好？ （reason 1，又 reason 2）

6. 你明年还想不想到中国来学中文？ （一方面…，一方面…）

II. Fill in the blank using the appropriate word from the list.

> 长途 预报 电视 借口
> 条件 兴奋 空调 安全

1. 你没有准时到机场，就应该道歉（dàoqiàn, apologize），别
   找 _____ 。

2. 天气 _____ 说今年夏天会很热，所以我想买个 _____ 。

3. 最近校园里问题很多，不太 _____ ，我妈妈担心得很。

4. 现在家家（jiājiā, every household）都有 _____ ，已经不是很特
   别的东西了。

5. _____ 电话很便宜（pián.yi, cheap），所以我常常给北京的朋
   友打电话。

III. Make a sentence with the underlined structures.

1. 宿舍里<u>不但</u>有空调，<u>还</u>有电视、电话和热水。

2. 听说这个校园安全<u>得很</u>，<u>而且</u>非常方便。

3. 你去了北京，<u>又</u>有那么好的条件，<u>要是再</u>学不好汉语，<u>可就</u>
   没有借口<u>了</u>。

4. 住得舒服一点儿<u>才</u>能好好儿学习啊！

IV. Complete the dialogues with the expressions provided.

1. A：对不起，我们旅馆里已经没有单人间了！

   B：什么？ _____。（简直）

2. A：这家商店又没有毛巾，又没有肥皂（féizào, soap），真是太不方便了！

   B：_____。（adj. 是 adj.，可是/不过…；A 离 B 近/远）

3. A：整理床铺只是一件小事情，你为什么不自己整理呢？

   B：_____。（听起来，A 比 B 还 adj.）

V. Translate into Chinese.

1. Yes, health is very important (重要, zhòngyào), but it should not be an excuse for not studying hard. If you keep on neglecting your studies, I am afraid that you will not be able to learn Chinese well.

2. He was spoiled by his parents. After he got to college, he could neither get along with his roommates, nor take care of himself. Nothing (in his life) is on track.

3. I don't know if I want to attend this university. On the one hand the learning environment (conditions) at this school is very good, but on the other hand it is said that the campus is not safe at all.

VI. Composition

Overseas students in America often complain that schools don't take good care of them. As an overseas student here in China, do you find that the same thing is happening to you, or is it true that foreign students are treated better in China? Now that you have had the experience of being an international student, what has been the newest thing for you? What has been the most difficult?

第三课　早起、洗澡

　　到了北京以后，早上七点半就⑴开始上课，我真不习惯。我在美国上大学，从来没⑵这么早起来过。九点钟的课还⑶常常迟到，更⑷不用说七点半的课了。

　　因为我喜欢晚睡，早起对我就特别困难。中国人

早起	zǎoqǐ	v.	get up early
洗澡	xǐ//zǎo	v.-o.	have a bath; bathe 洗: wash
开始	kāishǐ	v.	start; begin
习惯	xíguàn	v./n.	be accustomed to; be used to, habit; custom 我已经习惯每天早起早睡了。
上	shàng	v.	go to; be engaged (in work, study, etc.) at a fixed time 上中文课/上大学
从来没 v. 过	cónglái méi V. guò		have never V-ed before 从来没看见过/从来没吃过
迟到	chídào	v.	be late (for a fixed schedule or appointment) 上课不能迟到。 (迟到 is used for human actions only, and cannot take on an object.)
更	gèng	adv.	even more; more; still more
不用说	búyòngshuō	conj.	not to mention; needless to say
晚睡	wǎnshuì	v.	go to bed late
困难	kùnnán	adj./n.	difficult; difficulty

常说早晨头脑最清楚，是学习最好的时候。可对我

来说(5)，早上刚(6)起来的时候头脑最不清楚，需要

喝两三杯咖啡才能完全醒过来(7)。我真不懂为什么

得这么早上课。

　　中国人也常说：早睡早起身体好。我却(8)觉得起

得早晚跟身体健康没有什么关系(9)。不过，我现在是每

天晚睡早起，整天都累得要命(10)。

　　除了早起以外(11)，中国人晚上洗澡的习惯也是我

早晨	zǎo.chen	n.	morning
头脑	tóunǎo	n.	brains; mind (It is not used for the physical brain.) 脑: brain 头脑不清楚/很有头脑
清楚	qīng.chu	adj.	clear
可	kě	adv.	but; 可是
刚	gāng	adv.	just
需要	xūyào	v./n.	need; want; require 我需要一支笔。/我需要早点儿起来。
咖啡	kāfēi	n.	coffee
醒	xǐng	v.	wake up; sober up
懂	dǒng	v.	understand; comprehend; know
身体	shēntǐ	n.	body; health
却	què	adv.	but; yet; however
整天	zhěngtiān	adv.	the whole day; all day long
adj.得要命	….de yàomìng		awfully; extremely
除了…以外	chú.le … yǐwài		except for; aside from

到了北京以后才⑿发现的。一般来说⒀，美国人经常早
上洗澡，中国人却喜欢在晚上洗澡，所以中国的学生
宿舍多半儿是在晚饭以后、睡觉以前提供热水。我本
来⒁总是早上洗澡，来了中国以后，不得不⒂改成⒃晚
上洗澡了。以前我觉得，早上洗完澡，干干净净⒄的，
开始一天的工作很不错。现在我认为，晚上洗完澡，
舒舒服服地睡觉也很好。

　　来中国以前，我从来没想过早上洗澡好还是晚上
洗澡好。有许多事情，我本来以为⒅一定是这样做的，

发现	fāxiàn	*v.*	find; discover
一般来说	yìbān lái shuō	*adv.*	generally speaking
经常	jīngcháng	*adv.*	often; frequently
多半儿	duōbànr	*adv.*	mostly
提供	tígōng	*v.*	offer; provide; supply
本来	běnlái	*adv.*	originally; at first
总是	zǒngshì	*adv.*	always
不得不	bùdébù	*adv.*	have no choice but to; have to
改	gǎi	*v.*	change; alter; correct
成	chéng	*comp.*	into; become
干净	gānjìng	*adj.*	clean; neat and tidy
认为	rènwéi	*v.*	think; consider; hold
以为	yǐwéi	*v.*	mistakenly think
事情	shì.qing	*n.*	thing
一定	yídìng	*adv./adj.*	definitely, definite

到了中国，却发现中国人不一定这样做。我学会了从
另(19)一个角度看事情，这就是到外国去的好处。

学会	xué//huì	v.-c.	learn 他一到中国，就学会了怎么用筷子吃饭。
另	lìng	adj.	the other; another
角度	jiǎodù	n.	angle; point of view
外国	wàiguó	n.	foreign country
好处	hǎo.chu	n.	benefit; gain; profit; advantage

★ 繁體字課文 (fántǐzì kèwén, Text in Traditional Characters)

　　到了北京以後，早上七點半就(1)開始上課，我真
不習慣。我在美國上大學，從來沒(2)這麼早起來過。九
點鐘的課還(3)常常遲到，更(4)不用說七點半的課了。

　　因為我喜歡晚睡，早起對我就特別困難。中國
人常說早晨頭腦清楚，是學習最好的時候。可對我來
說(5)，早上剛(6)起來的時候頭腦最不清楚，需要喝兩三
杯咖啡才能完全醒過來(7)。我真不懂為什麼得這麼早上
課。

　　中國人也常說：早睡早起身體好。我卻(8)覺得起
得早晚跟身體健康沒有什麼關係(9)。不過，我現在是每
天晚睡早起，整天都累得要命(10)。

27

除了早起以外⑾，中國人晚上洗澡的習慣也是我到了北京以後才⑿發現的。一般來說⒀，美國人經常早上洗澡，中國人卻喜歡在晚上洗澡，所以中國的學生宿舍多半兒是在晚飯以後、睡覺以前提供熱水。我本來⒁總是早上洗澡，來了中國以後，不得不⒂改成⒃晚上洗澡了。

以前我覺得，早上洗完澡，乾乾淨淨⒄的，開始一天的工作很不錯。現在我認為，晚上洗完澡，舒舒服服地睡覺也很好。

來中國以前，我從來沒想過早上洗澡好還是晚上洗澡好。有許多事情，我本來以為⒅一定是這樣做的；到了中國，卻發現中國人不一定這樣做。我學會了從另⒆一個角度看事情，這就是到外國去的好處。

᜵ 语法点（yǔfǎdiǎn, Grammar Notes）

(1) 早上七点半**就**开始上课。
Classes start promptly at 7:30 am.

就 used after a word or phrase denoting time indicates that it is early or that something or someone is quick, or that the time concerned is short. 就 is pronounced in the neutral one with stress on the time word or phrase.

1. 我们明天就走。
We will leave tomorrow.

2. 你们先去，我马上就来。
You go first, and I will come immediately.

3. 他只学了一年就说得很好了。
He already speaks very well after having studied for only one year.

(2) 我**从来没**这么早起来**过**。

I have never gotten up so early.

从来 indicates that something has remained unchanged throughout time, from the past to the present. It implies a sense of emphatic negation. 从来没 *v.* 过 implies that the action has not happened in the past, although it might happen in the future. 从来不 *v.* suggests that the subject has a kind of policy or resolve that has prevented action in the past and probably will continue to prevent it in the future.

1. 我从来没打过国际长途电话。

I have never made an international call.

2. 我一喝咖啡肚子就不舒服，所以我从来不喝咖啡。

My stomach gets upset whenever I drink coffee, so I never drink it.

(3) 九点钟的课**还**常常迟到，更**不用说**七点半的课了。

I was often late even for 9 o'clock class, not to mention the 7:30 class.

When citing an extreme case, use 还 to convey the notion that even such a case does not satisfy the conditions stated, let alone anything else. It is always followed by a second clause that uses 不用说 or a rhetorical question such as 怎么…呢, 哪儿…呢.

1. 老师还看不懂这篇文章，更不用说我了。

Even the teacher cannot understand this article, not to mention myself.

2. 我连功课还做不完，哪儿有时间看电影呢！

I cannot even finish my homework; how would I have time to see a movie?

3. 中文考试总是很难，我好好儿地预备还考不好，怎么能不预备呢？

Chinese quizzes are always so difficult. I do poorly even when I prepare for them; how could I not prepare?

(4) 九点钟的课还常常迟到，**更**不用说七点半的课了。

更, meaning "even more" or "more," is used in a comparative clause to indicate that the subject is going to be or already is of a greater extent or degree than the things to which it is compared.

1. 我的头脑早晨不太清楚，晚上更不清楚。

My mind is not clear in the morning; it is even worse in the evening.

2. 学外国话比学别的更需要练习。

One has to practice even more when studying a foreign language than when studying anything else.

3. 现在你住在外国，更需要注意健康。

Now that you are living in a foreign country, you need to pay even more attention to your health.

(5) **对我来说**，早上刚起来的时候头脑最不清楚。

As for myself, my mind is most unclear when I have just gotten up in the morning.

对…来说 indicates the person or thing to whom or to which a statement pertains.

1. 对我来说，食堂离宿舍近很重要。

It is very important to me that the dining hall is close to the dormitory.

2. 对学习语言来说，听录音带特别有帮助。

Listening to tapes is especially helpful in studying a foreign language.

(6) 对我来说，早上**刚**起来的时候头脑最不清楚。

刚 is an adverb which indicates that an action has recently occurred.

1. 我刚到北京的时候，常打电话给父母，现在不常打了。

When I first arrived in Beijing I called my parents frequently, but I don't call them often anymore.

2. 昨天我刚到学校，就看见了外事处的张先生。

When I had just arrived at school yesterday, I saw Mr. Zhang from the Foreign Affairs Office.

(7) 需要喝两三杯咖啡才能完全醒**过来**。

I need to drink two or three cups of coffee to really wake up.

V. 过来 usually indicates that someone or something is approaching, e.g. 走过来, 跑过来. But when it is used after certain verbs, such as 醒 or 明白, it means that the subject has returned to the original and normal situation.

1. 我说了好几次，他才明白过来。

He understood only after I explained it several times.

2. 要是他早晨不喝咖啡，就醒不过来。

   If he doesn't drink coffee in the morning, he never really wakes up.

(8) 中国人常说：早睡早起身体好。我**却**觉得起得早晚跟身体健康没有什么关系。

Chinese people always say that early to bed early to rise makes one healthy. I, however, still think that there is no relation between waking up early or late and one's health.

却 is an adverb inserted between the subject and predicate of a sentence. Its function of indicating contrast is similar to that of 但是,可是, and 不过。It can be used with these conjunctions to intensify contrast.

1. 北京是一个古老的城市，但是北京的高速公路却很新。

   Beijing is an old city, but its highways are pretty new.

2. 我很累，可是却睡不着觉。

   I was very tired, but I couldn't sleep.

(9) 我却觉得起得早晚**跟**身体健康**没有什么关系**。

   A 跟 B 有/没有关系 means "A has/has nothing to do with B."

1. 我跟这件事情完全没有关系，你别问我。

   I have nothing to do with this matter. Don't ask me.

2. 一个人的生活习惯和他是哪儿的人很有关系。

   One's living habits have a lot to do with the place from which one comes.

(10) 我整天都累**得要命**。

I was terribly tired the whole day.

要命 literally means "to drive somebody to his death." The structure *adj.* 得要命 means "extremely/awfully adjective." It is usually used in an undesirable situation.

1. 去年夏天，北京热得要命。

   Beijing was terribly hot last summer.

2. 我累得要命，得休息休息。

   I am terribly tired. I need to rest for a while.

(11) **除了**早起**以外**，中国人晚上洗澡的习惯**也**是我到了北京以后才发现的。

Only after I arrived in Beijing did I learn that, besides getting up early, Chinese people are also accustomed to taking a bath in the evening.

除了 is often used in conjunction with 以外. When 除了… （以外） is followed by 也 or 还, it means "in addition to" or "besides."

1. 除了学习以外，我们也常一块儿出去玩。
   In addition to studying, we often go out to have fun together.

2. 除了书以外，我还买了两条毛巾。
   In addition to books, I bought two towels.

When 除了… （以外） is followed by 都 or a negative construction, it means "except."

3. 除了我以外，别人都晚上洗澡。
   All the others take baths in the evening except me.

4. 教室里除了几个学生以外，没有别人。
   There were no others in the classroom except for a few students.

(12) 中国人晚上洗澡的习惯也是我到了北京以后**才**发现的。

This 才 is different from the one in L. 2, Note (11). In this lesson, 才 is used after a word or a phrase to denote a time which is later than expected or of long duration. In this usage, 才 is pronounced in the neutral tone and the time expression is stressed. It may be applied either to a fulfilled or an unfulfilled event. 才 sometimes implies "not until" or "only then."

1. 我得做完功课才能跟你谈话。
   I have to finish my homework before I can talk with you.

2. 我今天才知道他不是中国人。
   I didn't know that he was not Chinese until today.

(13) **一般来说**，美国人经常早上洗澡。

Generally speaking, Americans take baths in the morning.

一般来说 means "generally speaking." It is the same as 一般说来.

1. 一般来说，中国人先吃饭再喝汤，美国人却不是这样。
   Generally speaking, Chinese people eat first and then have soup, but American people don't do it this way.

2. 一般来说，美国学生宿舍的大门是不锁的。

Generally speaking, in America, the main entrances of student dorms are left unlocked.

(14) 我**本来**总是早上洗澡。

I used to take baths in the morning.

本来 means "originally," implying that the situation has changed.

1. 我本来想给他打电话，后来给他写了一封信。

I originally planned to call him, but later I wrote him a letter instead.

2. 海关的检查本来很严，可是现在特别松。

Customs inspection used to be strict, but it is very lax now.

(15) 来了中国以后，**不得不**改成晚上洗澡了。

After I came to China, I had to change over to taking baths in the evening.

不得不 means "to have no choice but to" or "to have to." It is used as an adverbial expression.

1. 没有人到机场接我，我不得不自己坐车到学校去。

There was no one to pick me up in the airport, so I had to take a bus to school on my own.

2. 今年夏天特别热，我不得不买个空调。

It is so hot this summer that I have no choice but to buy an air conditioner.

(16) 来了中国以后，不得不改**成**晚上洗澡了。

成 is a resultative complement which is used after verbs to convey the sense of "becoming" or "being completed." It is often used in conjunction with the 把 construction.

1. 你帮我把这件事办成以后，我一定要请你吃饭。

I will be sure to treat you to dinner after you help me complete this job.

2. 你不应该把住在外国说成是一件那么可怕的事。

You shouldn't describe living in a foreign country as such a terrifying thing.

(17) 早上洗完澡，**干干净净的**，开始一天的工作很不错。

It is not bad taking a shower in the morning and starting the day's work cleanly (with a clean feeling).

干干净净 is an adjective created by duplicating the adjective 干净 in an AABB pattern for emphasis. Such a pattern can be used as an adjective or an adverb. In spoken language a 的 or 地 is added after the AABB syllable, e.g. 舒舒服服地坐着, or 高高兴兴地回了家.

(18) 有许多事情，我本来**以为**一定是这样做的。

There were many things that I thought had to be done this way.

以为 means "to think," usually implying "to think incorrectly."

1. 我以为从机场到学校很远，其实只要半个钟头。

I thought that the school was very far from the airport, but actually it only took half an hour.

2. 他以为中国的海关查得很严，其实查得很松。

He thought that China's customs was strict, but it was actually lax.

(19) 我学会了从**另**一个角度看事情。

I learned to look at things from another angle.

When 另 or 另外 modifies a noun, it is a demonstrative pronoun indicating something other than what has been mentioned. It differs with 别的 in that 另 or 另外 can be followed by a number + *AN*, meaning "the one or few in particular," while 别的 indicates others in general. Compare the following two sentences:

1. 这间屋子太热，他搬到另外一间去了。

This room is too hot. He has moved to another room.

2. 我觉得这间不够大，能不能看看别的屋子？

I think that this room is not big enough. Can I have a look at others?

✎ 练习（liànxí, Exercise）

I. Answer the following questions using the expressions when provided.

1. 刚到中国的时候，你有没有时差的问题？你习惯不习惯中国的生活？（…得要命）

2. 你上课常常迟到吗？（从来没 v. 过）

3. 你喜欢在北京学习吗？除了学习以外，有没有时间出去玩呢？（连…都…，更不用说…）

4. 你认为学习好不好跟住的条件有没有关系？

5. 你不是天天喝咖啡吗？现在怎么喝起茶来了？（不得不）

6. 中国海关的检查严不严？（本来以为…）

7. 你跟父母关系好不好？他们是你的朋友吗？（把…看成…）

8. 有什么事情你本来以为一定是这样做，到了中国却发现中国人不一定这样做？

II. Make a sentence using the underlined expression.

1. <u>对我来说</u>，早上刚起来的时候头脑最不清楚。

2. <u>一般来说</u>，美国人经常早上洗澡，中国人却喜欢晚上洗澡。

3. <u>除了</u>早起<u>以外</u>，中国人晚上洗澡的习惯<u>也</u>是我到了北京以后才发现的。

4. 我学会了<u>从另一个角度</u>看事情，这就是到外国去的好处。

III. Choose the correct answer.

1. 要是你不想去，你应该明明白白 _____ 告诉我。
   ① 的　② 地　③ 得　④ 着

2. 我 _____ 你应该努力学习，不应该找借口。
   ① 认为　② 以为　③ 学会　④ 喜欢

3. 我到了中国以后，_____ 打过电话。
   ① 从来给父母不　② 从来给父母打
   ③ 从来没给父母　④ 不从来给父母

4. 你要是带了花花公子杂志，就 _____ 通过海关。
   ① 很难　② 有困难　③ 困难得很　④ 难一点儿

IV. Complete the dialogues with the expressions provided.

1. A: 外国学生宿舍，又有空调又有电视，我认为学校太照顾外国学生了。

   B: _____。（对…来说）

2. A: 我想在吃晚饭以前洗个热水澡。不知道宿舍里有没有热水？

   B: _____。（…以后，才…）

3. A: 你现在能看中文杂志了吗？

   B: _____。（还…，更不用说…）

4. A: 你为什么不坐张先生的车到机场去？却坐出租车(chūzūchē, taxi)去呢？

   B: _____。（本来…，可是…；不得不）

V. Translate into Chinese.

1. Going abroad has one benefit, which is that one can learn to look at things from another perspective. There were many customs which I had originally thought were a certain way, but after going to China, I finally realized that some customs are completely different from what I had imagined.

2. I have class at 8:00 in the morning, but I like sleeping late, so waking up early is particularly difficult for me. I am often not completely awake by 8:00; it is not even worth talking about getting to class on time.

3. I have never liked showering in the evening. If I shower at night, I cannot sleep and will be incredibly tired the next day. After I take a shower in the morning, not only can I start the day's work cleanly, but my mind is also clear. I feel that when one takes a shower is related to whether his work goes smoothly or not.

VI. Composition

Chinese people believe that early to bed and early to rise is good for one's health. According to a Western saying, "The early bird catches the worm." Do you agree with these beliefs? Why? What is your daily schedule? Is it the best schedule for you? Are these beliefs still applicable in our modern society where everybody works at a different pace?

第五课　　拉肚子、睡不好

学生：王老师，今天我觉得很不舒服，想请半天假，

在宿舍里休息休息。

老师：怎么了⑴？是不是病了？

学生：昨天晚上我吃了一碗牛肉面，一块西瓜。睡觉

以前，肚子很疼，拉了好几次，后来还吐了。

肚子	dù.zi	n.	stomach; abdomen
拉肚子	lā dù.zi	v.-o.	suffer from diarrhea; have loose bowels
请假	qǐng//jià	v.-o.	ask for leave 请了三天假
休息	xiū.xi	v.	rest; have a rest
病	bìng	v.	be sick; be ill 他病得很厉害，不能来上课。 (To say "a little sick," use 有点不舒服. Don't put any modifiers before the word 病.)
碗	wǎn	AN/n.	bowl
牛肉	niúròu	n.	beef 肉: meat
面	miàn	n.	noodle
块	kuài	AN	piece; lump; chunk 一块鸡肉
西瓜	xīguā	n.	watermelon
疼	téng	v./adj.	ache, sore; painful
吐	tù	v.	vomit

老师：也许你吃的东西不大(2)干净。发烧了没有？

学生：烧倒(3)是(4)没烧，可是没睡好觉。这几个星期我天天都睡不好，累极了。

老师：为什么总睡不好呢？

学生：宿舍里太热了。

老师：不是有空调吗(5)？

学生：我同屋不喜欢开空调，喜欢开窗。结果(6)屋子里蚊子多得要命。昨天晚上我被叮了好几次。你看，脸上、胳膊上都是包(7)。

老师：我不知道你们有这样的问题。我看，你们得好好儿谈谈。

也许	yěxǔ	*adv.*	maybe; perhaps
发烧	fā//shāo	*v.-o.*	have a fever
			发了两天烧/烧得很厉害
倒	dào	*adv.*	on the contrary
总	zǒng	*adv.*	总是; always
结果	jiéguǒ	*adv./n.*	as a result, result
蚊子	wén.zi	*n.*	mosquito
叮	dīng	*v.*	sting; bite
脸	liǎn	*n.*	(said of people or animals) face
胳膊	gē.bo	*n.*	arm
包	bāo	*n.*	swelling; lump
问题	wèntí	*n.*	trouble; problem; question

学生：谈过好几次了。但是他总是把窗子开开，把空
　　　调关掉(8)。我们的关系越来越(9)紧张了。

老师：这件事，我真不知道(10)该怎么帮你的忙。你先到
　　　学校的医院去，让大夫看看吧！

好几…	hǎo jǐ…		quite a few
			好几个人/好几天/好几杯咖啡
开开	kāi//.kāi	v.-c.	"open-open"; 打开; open; turn on
			把窗户开开/把电视打开
关掉	guān//diào	v.-c.	turn off 把电视关掉
越来越…	yuè lái yuè…		more and more…
紧张	jǐnzhāng	adj.	tense; intense; strained
该	gāi	aux.	should; ought to; 应该
帮忙	bāng//máng	v.-o.	help
			帮朋友的忙/帮我把那本书拿过来
医院	yīyuàn	n.	hospital
大夫	dài.fu	n.	physician; doctor

★ 繁体字课文 (fántǐzì kèwén, Text in Traditional Characters)

學生：王老師，今天我覺得很不舒服，想請半天假，
　　　在宿舍裏休息休息。

老師：怎麼了(1)？是不是病了？

學生：昨天晚上我吃了一碗牛肉麵，一塊西瓜。睡覺
　　　以前，肚子很疼，拉了好幾次，後來還吐了。

老師：也許你吃的東西不大(2)乾淨。發燒了沒有？

學生：燒倒(3)是(4)沒燒，可是沒睡好覺。這幾個星期我
　　　天天都睡不好，累極了。

老師：為什麼總睡不好呢？

學生：宿舍裏太熱了。

老師：不是有空調嗎(5)？

學生：我同屋不喜歡開空調，喜歡開窗。結果(6)屋子裏蚊子多得要命。昨天晚上我被叮了好幾次。你看，臉上、胳膊上都是包(7)。

老師：我不知道你們有這樣的問題。我看，你們得好好兒談談。

學生：談過好幾次了。但是他總是把窗子開開，把空調關掉(8)。我們的關係越來越(9)緊張了。

老師：這件事，我真不知道(10)該怎麼幫你的忙。你先到學校的醫院去，讓大夫看看吧！

᧝ 语法点（yǔfǎdiǎn, Grammar Notes）

(1) **怎么了** means "what happened?" or "what's the matter?."

(2) 也许你吃的东西**不大**干净。

It could be that the things you ate were not very clean.

不大 means "not often," "seldom," "not too" or "not very." It can be followed by an adjective, as in the above example, or it can be followed by a verb, such as 不大喜欢, 不大高兴, 不大明白. In this way, it has a similar meaning to 不太. However, 不大 also indicates that the subject does not meet a certain expectation. 太 can serve independently as "too" (太早, 太紧张, 太贵), whereas 大 cannot function independently without 不.

1. 我不大清楚邮局在哪儿，你最好去问问别人。

I don't know exactly where the post office is. You'd better ask someone else.

2. 坐公共汽车不大方便，还是坐出租车吧！

It is not very convenient to get there by bus. Let's take a taxi.

3. 他不大看电影。

He seldom watches movies.

4. 我不大想到那儿去。

I am not very keen on going there.

(3) 烧**倒**是没烧，可是没睡好觉。

I don't actually have fever, but I didn't sleep well.

倒 is an adverb used to indicate that the outcome of something is exactly opposite to what it should be or what one has expected.

1. 到了北京以后，人人都很兴奋，我倒担心起来。

After arriving in Beijing, everybody got excited, but I started to worry.

2. 在北京，什么都很便宜，可是国际长途电话倒比美国贵得多。

Everything is very inexpensive in Beijing, but international calls are much more expensive than those in America.

(4) 烧**倒**是没烧，**可是**没睡好觉。

This pattern is the same as "…是…，可是…" in Lesson 2, Note (2). 倒 is optional, 是 is also optional. Therefore, it is correct to say both "…是…，可是…" and "…倒…，可是…."

(5) **不是**有空调**吗**？

Isn't there air conditioning in your dorm?

不是…吗 is a rhetorical question.

1. 你对海关的印象不是很好吗？

Don't you have a good impression of Chinese customs?

2. 校园里不是很安全吗？你为什么要住在学校外头呢？

Isn't the campus safe? Why do you want to live outside of the school?

(6) 他喜欢开窗。**结果**屋子里蚊子多得要命。

He likes to have the windows opened. As a result, there are an awful lot of mosquitoes in the room.

结果 is used as an adverb here, meaning "as a result" or "consequently." Very often it introduces an undesirable result.

1. 他吃了不干净的东西，结果拉了好几天肚子。

He ate unclean food, and as a result, had diarrhea for several days.

2. 他请假请得太多，结果考试考得很差。

He asked for too many days leave, and as a result, he tested poorly on his examination.

(7) 我脸上、胳膊上**都是**包。

I have these (lumps) over my face and arms (and everywhere).

The pattern is: place word + 都是 + *n.*. The noun can be dropped if it is understood. This pattern implies exaggeration.

1. 她的书太多，桌子上、椅子上、床上都是。

She has too many books. They are on her desk, her chairs, her bed and everywhere.

2. 外头都是中国学生，怎么会没有机会说中国话呢？

There are a lot of Chinese students out there. How could there be no chance to speak Chinese?

(8) 他总是把窗子开开，把空调关**掉**。

He always opened the window, and turned off the air conditioning.

关掉 means "to turn off." 掉 means "to fall off" or "to lose." When used as a resultative complement, it indicates that the object does not exist any longer after the verb is completed; e.g. 把这块西瓜吃掉, 把电视关掉, 用掉了多少钱. Review these resultative complements from previous lessons: 打开, 睡着, 惯坏, 学好, 寄丢, 睡好, 开开.

(9) 我们的关系**越来越**紧张了。

Our relationship is becoming more and more strained.

越来越 functions as an adverbial indicating the increasing intensity in degree of the adjective following it.

1. 他努力学习，成绩越来越好了。

He studies hard, and his grades are getting better and better.

2. 到中国来学中文的外国人越来越多了。

There are more and more foreigners coming to China to study Chinese.

越…越… is also used with words, phrases, or clauses to indicate that the second state of affairs advances in step with its preceding state.

3. 天气越热，用空调的人就越多。

The hotter it gets, the more people there are who use air conditioning.

4. 你练习得越多，就写得越好看。
The more you practice, the better you'll write.

⑽ 我真**不知道**该怎么帮你的忙。
I really don't know how to help you.

What follows 知道 could be 1) a noun or a sentence; e.g. 他知道你的名字；我不知道宿舍里没有空调；2) a clause asking how, who, why, when, where, etc.; e.g. 你知道不知道老师什么时候来？我真不知道该怎么帮你的忙；3) (after the negative verb "不知道" only) a clause with "if" in English; e.g. I don't know if they sell scenery postcards. "我不知道他们卖不卖风景明信片." Please note that you should use v. 不 v., v. 了没有, or 是 A 还是 B instead of using 要是 in a "S. do/does not know if …" sentence.

1. 你知道不知道他们的关系为什么这么紧张？
Do you know why their relationship is so strained?

2. 我不知道她是中国人还是美国人。
I don't know if she is Chinese or American.

3. 我不知道附近有没有邮局。你问问服务员吧！
I don't know if there is a post office nearby. Go ask the receptionist.

4. 我不知道飞机降落了没有。
I don't know if the airplane has landed or not.

✎ 练习（**liànxí**, Exercise）

I. Answer the following questions using the structures provided.

1. 你昨天不是还很好吗？怎么今天病了呢？（…，结果…）

2. 北京的生活怎么样？你喜欢吗？（…得要命）

3. 你到北京来以后，跟朋友说过英文吗？（…倒是…，可是…）

4. 你常在校园外的小饭馆吃饭吗？（不大…，因为）

5. 寄国际挂号比较快吗？（我不知道…）

6. 你跟你同屋的关系好不好？（越来越…）

7. 这间屋子怎么这么热？空调不是已经开了吗？（以为，把…）

8. 听说你昨天发烧了？ （后来）

II. Correct the underlined errors.

1. <u>他越来越病了</u>，得去看大夫。

2. 我昨天晚上<u>拉了两个肚子</u>，一夜都没睡好。

3. 请你<u>把窗户关</u>，屋子里的蚊子太多了。

4. <u>我们的关系是紧张</u>，总是谈不来。

5. 明天我想请一天假，<u>休一天息</u>。

III. Complete the dialogues with the expressions provided.

1. A：你的同屋是不是把空调开得太冷（lěng, cold）了？

   B：_____。 （倒是，可是）

2. A：你要明信片还是邮票？

   B：_____。 （A，B 都…）

3. A：我觉得有点儿冷。空调还开着吗？

   B：_____。 （把…v. 掉）

4. A：你去过他的屋子吗？他经常整理吗？

   B：他的屋子太乱了！ _____。 （place word ＋都是 n.）

IV. Translate into Chinese.

1. Because of his fever, he took the morning off yesterday to see the campus doctor. However, he vomited and had diarrhea several times last night. As a result, he did not test (考试 [v.-o.], kǎoshì) well in class today.

2. There are an awful lot of mosquitoes in this dormitory, so I told the foreign affairs office that it would be better if we could turn on the air conditioning at night.

3. I know you cannot sleep well at night because your roommate goes to bed late. Over the past few days, I have been thinking about how to help you. As I see it, we have to talk over the matter with him thoroughly.

V. Composition

   As an international student, would you prefer living with someone from your country, having a home stay with a Chinese family, or living with Chinese students in the dormitory? Can you point out the advantages and disadvantages of these three options?

第六课　睡午觉、喝热水

中国人多半儿在中饭以后睡个午觉。刚到北京的时候，我很不习惯。怎么⑴白天睡觉呢？不是太浪费时间了吗？但是两个星期以后，我自己⑵也睡起午觉来⑶了。

我们早上七点半就开始上课，中饭以后已经⑷很累了。休息半个小时，让⑸我下午和晚上都比较有精神。怪不得⑹中国人大多有睡午觉的习惯。

一般说来，中国人喜欢喝热茶，很少喝冰水。夏天

午觉	wǔjiào	_n._	afternoon nap
白天	báitiān	_n._	daytime; day
浪费	làngfèi	_v./adj._	waste; squander, extravagant 浪费时间/浪费钱/太浪费了
自己	zìjǐ	_pron._	oneself 你自己/我自己/他自己
精神	jīng.shen	_n._	vigor; vitality; spirit
有精神	yǒu jīng.shen	_adj._	vigorous 很有精神/没有什么精神
怪不得	guài.bu.de	_conj._	no wonder; so that's why
大多	dàduō	_adv._	for the most part; mostly
茶	chá	_n._	tea
很少	hěnshǎo	_adv._	seldom
冰水	bīngshuǐ	_n._	ice water　　冰: ice

喝热水，对我来说，简直是受罪！但是因为中国的自来水不能直接喝，要喝到凉开水并(7)不容易。每天买矿泉水不但贵也不方便，所以最近我学着(8)喝热水瓶里的热水，有时也泡茶。没想到(9)喝了几天以后，我也习惯了，而且觉得热水并不难喝呢！

受罪	shòu//zuì	v.-o.	endure hardships, tortures, rough condition, etc.; have a hard time 受: receive; suffer 罪: sin; hardship
自来水	zìláishuǐ	n.	tap water
直接	zhíjiē	adv.	directly
凉	liáng	adj.	cold; cool
开水	kāishuǐ	n.	boiled water
容易	róngyì	adj.	easy
矿泉水	kuàngquánshuǐ	n.	mineral water 矿泉: mineral spring
贵	guì	adj.	expensive
最近	zuìjìn	adv.	recently
学	xué	v.	imitate; mimic
热水瓶	rèshuǐpíng	n.	thermos bottle 瓶: bottle
有时	yǒushí	adv.	有时候; sometimes; at times; now and then 我常常喝冰水，有时也喝热茶。
泡茶	pào//chá	v.-o.	make tea 泡: brew
没想到	méi xiǎngdào	adv.	unexpectedly

　　各地有各地的习惯，这都是有原因的。我们到一个新地方，不应该再坚持自己原来的生活方式，得向⑩当地人学习才行。

各 *n.*	gè	*adj.*	each; every 各人有各人的想法。
原因	yuányīn	*n.*	reason; cause
坚持	jiānchí	*v.*	insist on; persist in
原来	yuánlái	*adj.*	original, former
生活	shēnghuó	*n.*	life
方式	fāngshì	*n.*	pattern; fashion; way
向	xiàng	*prep.*	from
当地	dāngdì	*p.w.*	local; in the locality

★ 繁体字课文（fántǐzì kèwén）

　　中國人多半儿在中飯以後睡個午覺。剛到北京的時候，我很不習慣。怎麼⑴白天睡覺呢？不是太浪費時間了嗎？但是兩個星期以後，我自己⑵也睡起午覺來⑶了。

　　我們早上七點半就開始上課，中飯以後已經⑷很累了。休息半個小時，讓⑸我下午和晚上都比較有精神。怪不得⑹中國人大多有睡午覺的習慣。

　　一般說來，中國人喜歡喝熱茶，很少喝冰水。夏天喝熱水，對我來說，簡直是受罪！但是因為中國的自來水不能直接喝，要喝到涼開水並⑺不容易。每天買礦泉水不但貴也不方便，所以最近我學著⑻喝熱水

瓶裏的熱水，有時也泡茶。沒想到⑼喝了幾天以後，
我也習慣了，而且覺得熱水並不難喝呢！

　　各地有各地的習慣，這都是有原因的。我們到一
個新地方，不應該再堅持自己原來的生活方式，得向⑽
當地人學習才行。

⌇ 语法点（yǔfǎdiǎn）

(1) **怎么**白天睡觉呢？
How come they sleep during the day?

　　怎么 here indicates puzzlement.

　1. 你怎么不在屋子里看书？怎么到这儿来了？
　　　How come you are not studying in your room? Why did you come
　　　here?

　2. 怎么？他到现在还没有中文名字吗？
　　　What? He still doesn't have a Chinese name?

(2) 两个星期以后，我**自己**也睡起午觉来了。
After two weeks, I too began taking afternoon naps.

　　自己 is a reflexive pronoun. It often follows a pronoun and is used for
emphasis.

　1. 你不信我的话？那你自己去看看！
　　　You don't believe me? Then go and see for yourself!

　2. 这是你自己的事，我怎么能帮你的忙？
　　　This is your own business. How can I help?

(3) 两个星期以后，我自己也睡**起**午觉**来**了。

　　起来, following a verb or adjective used as the predicate in a sentence,
means "to start to" or "to become." When there is an object following the
verb, the pattern is v.起 o.来.

　1. 她小时候不怎么样，长大了却漂亮起来了。

She was nothing special when she was little, but she is a lot prettier now that she's older.

2. 不知道为什么，他生起气来了。

I don't know why he got angry.

(4) 中饭以后**已经**很累了。

After lunch I was already exhausted.

Usually 已经 indicates that an action has been completed. Here it indicates that the topic has already reached a certain degree, or implies that one can not do better or more. It can modify negative phrases.

1. 他已经快累死了，最好别叫他整理屋子了。

He is already exhausted. You'd best not to ask him to tidy up his room.

2. 我已经很忙了，没时间做别的事了。

I am already quite busy. I don't have time for anything else.

3. 写得对已经不容易了，要写得好就更难了。

It is already hard to write correctly. It is even harder to write so that it looks good.

(5) 休息半个小时，**让**我下午和晚上都比较有精神。

Resting for half an hour makes me more energetic in the afternoon and evening.

In this context 让 means "to make (a situation happen)."

1. 那么多学生迟到，让老师很生气。

The fact that so many students were late made the teacher very angry.

2. 他又吐又拉肚子，让他父母非常担心。

He was vomiting and has diarrhea, making his parents very worried.

(6) **怪不得**中国人大多有睡午觉的习惯。

No wonder most Chinese people are used to taking afternoon naps.

怪不得 most often modifies subject-predicate constructions or verbal phrases. The explanation may either precede or follow 怪不得.

1. 怪不得他天天到图书馆去，下星期就要考试了。

No wonder he goes to the library everyday. The exam is next week.

2. 早上七点半就开始上课了，怪不得学生都累得要命。

The class starts at 7:30 in the morning; no wonder the students are all extremely tired.

(7) 要喝到凉开水并不容易。

It is not that easy to get cold water.

并 is used before a negative form to indicate that a fact is not as one may think or expect. It can also be used to emphasize negative verbal phrases.

1. 打国际长途电话并没有想像中那么贵。

It is not as expensive as you might imagine to make an international call.

2. 邮局并不远，可以走路去。

The post office is not far. You can walk there.

(8) 最近我学着喝热水瓶里的热水。

I am learning to drink hot water from a thermos.

着 is used after a verb to indicate that an action is in progress; it is often used in conjunction with 正, 在, or similar adverbs.

1. 我到的时候，他正跟同屋谈着呢！

He was talking with his roommate when I arrived.

2. 我一进去，所有的人就都看着我。

As soon as I entered, everyone was looking at me.

(9) **没想到**喝了几天以后，我也习惯了。

Surprisingly, after drinking it for a few days, I got used to it too.

When 没想到 is preceded with a person or a personal pronoun as subject, e.g. 我没想到, 张先生没想到, it means "didn't expect." 我没想到他明天要来 means "I didn't expect that he would come tomorrow." It can also be used as an adverbial meaning "surprisingly" or "unexpectedly." In this case, 没想到 usually modifies a fulfilled event and comes before the subject.

1. 没想到北京是一个这么现代化的城市。

I never thought that Beijing would be such a modern city.

2. 没想到我们的宿舍非常大。

Unexpectedly, our dorm was very big.

(10) 我们不应该再坚持自己原来的生活方式，**得向**当地人学习才行。

We shouldn't insist on maintaining our original way of living; instead, we ought to learn form the locals.

向 means "(to try to get something) from." It can be replaced by 跟.

1. 他向父母要了很多钱，打算买一辆车。
   He asked for a lot of money from his parents to buy a car.

2. 中国每年都向外国买很多飞机、汽车。
   China buys many airplanes and cars from foreign countries every year.

✐ 练习（liànxí）

I. Answer the following questions using the structures when provided.

1. 在中国生活，除了喝热水以外，你有没有别的困难？（让）

2. 你现在有睡午觉的习惯吗？你认为睡午觉有什么好处？

3. 在中国的时候，你经常喝热茶吗？（大多，很少）

4. 你在中国和在美国的生活方式完全一样吗？（v. 起 o. 来）

5. 你觉得晚上睡觉的时候非开空调不可吗？（并不坚持）

II. Make a sentence using the underlined expression.

1. 夏天喝热水，<u>对我来说</u>，<u>简直是</u>受罪！

2. 我<u>最近学</u>着喝热水瓶里的热水，有时也泡茶。

3. 我们到了一个新地方，<u>得向当地人学习才行</u>。

4. 休息半个小时，<u>让</u>我下午和晚上都比较有精神。

III. Choose the correct answer.

1. 我到了中国以后，也学中国人_____了。
   ① 喝热茶起来　② 喝起来热茶
   ③ 喝起热茶来　④ 喝了起来热茶

2. 对我来说，喝冰水_____。
   ① 比较喝热水舒服　② 比较舒服
   ③ 比喝热水不舒服　④ 一点儿舒服

3. 要是你一天拉了好几次，那得去看大夫_____行。
   ① 才　② 就　③ 只　④ 倒

4. 他坚持自己_____ 的做法，不想向别人学习。

    ① 原来　② 大多　③ 多半儿　④ 好好儿

IV. Complete the dialogues with the expressions provided.

1. A：你为什么不让外事处的人带你到邮局去？

    B：_____。（已经…了，照顾）

2. A：我昨天晚上两点才睡觉。

    B：_____。（怪不得）

3. A：每天到饭馆儿吃饭不是很方便吗？

    B：_____。（并）

4. A：你现在有个中国朋友了，可以经常跟他说中文了！

    B：_____。（以为，没想到）

V. Translate into Chinese.

1. Since coming to China, the thing that bothers me most is that I can't drink cold boiled water (喝不到). At first I bought mineral water every day, but it was very expensive. Now I cannot do anything but switch to drinking hot water in a thermos.

2. Yesterday the air conditioner in our classroom broke (坏了, huàile). Not having air conditioning during the summer is simply torture for me. About 10 minutes after the class started, the students began to fall asleep. Unexpectedly, the teacher thought that we didn't like her class and started to lose her temper (生起气来).

3. A: How come you make tea so well?
B: There is a good reason. I lived in China for ten years and learned their method of making tea from one of my Chinese friends.
A: No wonder you know how to make tea.

VI. Composition

    Chinese people don't drink ice water, but Americans do. When one gets sick, Americans recommend drinking huge amounts of orange juice, while Chinese mothers keep their children from eating any oranges. Chinese people cook vegetables before they eat them, and Americans love eating raw vegetable salads. Can you find any other similar examples? Why do people in different places have such different philosophies about life? Can you say that one is right and the other is wrong?

第十课　讲价

（一）在古董店里

学生：这幅山水画儿多少钱啊？

老板：这幅画儿是明代的，现在世界上只有这一幅了。

学生：明代的？怎么看起来这么新呢？

老板：噢！我们重新(1)整理过，比原来的好多了。

学生：这幅画儿多少钱呢？

老板：现在明代的画儿越来越少了，我们只有这一幅

了……

讲价	jiǎng//jià	v.-o.	bargain; haggle over the price 价: 价钱; 价格; price
古董	gǔdǒng	n.	antique
幅	fú	AN	measure word for painting
山水画儿	shānshuǐhuàr	n.	landscape painting
老板	lǎobǎn	n.	shopkeeper; boss
明代	Míngdài	n.	the Ming Dynasty (1368-1644)
世界	shìjiè	n.	world
噢	o	interj.	oh (indicating understanding)
重新	chóngxīn	adv.	again; anew; afresh

学生：我知道这是古画儿，到底(2)要多少钱呢？

老板：我们对(3)外国朋友总是特别客气……

学生：你到底要多少钱啊？

老板：这幅画儿要是(4)在别的店里，要三千块。我卖给你，只要一千块就行了。

学生：一千块？太贵了！

老板：一千块是我的成本，我连一块钱都不赚。

学生：五百块，行不行？

老板：开玩笑！要是五百块卖给你，那我就赔五百块！

学生：我是个穷学生，根本买不起(5)一千块钱的画儿。再见再见！

古画儿	gǔhuàr	n.	ancient painting
到底	dàodǐ	adv.	after all; exactly
要是	yàoshì	conj.	if
成本	chéngběn	n.	cost
赚钱	zhuàn//qián	v.-o.	make money; make a profit 赚了一千块钱
开玩笑	kāi wánxiào	v.-o.	joke; make fun of 开别人玩笑/别开玩笑
赔钱	péi//qián	v.-o.	lose money (in business transaction) 赔了不少钱
穷	qióng	adj.	poor; poverty-stricken
买不起	mǎi .bu .qǐ	v.-c.	cannot afford positive form: 买得起

老板：来来来来来，别走别走！你觉得这幅太贵，我

　　　们有比较便宜的。你看这幅人物画儿……

学生：我不喜欢人物画儿。我就是(6)要这幅山水画儿。

　　　要是不便宜一点儿，我只好(7)不买了。

老板：别走别走！八百块卖给你了！

学生：太贵了！太贵了！我还有事儿，我得走了！

老板：七百块怎么样？

学生：我只有五百块钱，多一块都买不起！

老板：好吧好吧！五百块钱，卖给你了！

（二）在宿舍里

学生：我今天逛古董市场，买了一幅山水画儿，便宜

　　　极了。那个老板本来要一千块钱，后来五百块

　　　就卖给我了。

人物	rénwù	n.	figure; personage; character (in a novel, etc.)
便宜	pián.yi	adj.	inexpensive; cheap
只好	zhǐhǎo	adv.	have to; be forced to
逛	guàng	v.	stroll; go window-shopping
市场	shìchǎng	n.	market

同屋：真巧，我今天也在古董市场买了一幅画儿。

学生：给我看看！

同屋：我最喜欢山水画儿。你看这幅，真棒！

学生：哎呀！怎么跟我买的一模一样？你花了多少钱？

同屋：我才(8)花了一百块！

学生：糟糕！又(9)上当(10)了！

巧	qiǎo	*adj.*	coincidental; fortuitous
棒	bàng	*adj.*	(colloquial) good; excellent
哎呀	aīyā	*interj.*	Oh!; Ah! (It expresses anger, irritation, contempt or disappointment.)
一模一样	yìmú yíyàng	*adj.*	exactly alike 这个跟那个一模一样。
花钱	huā//qián	*v.-o.*	spend (money)
上当	shàng//dàng	*v.-o.*	be taken in; be fooled 上了那个老板的当 你别上他的当。

★ 繁体字课文 (fántǐzì kèwén)

（一）在古董店裏

學生：這幅山水畫儿多少錢啊？

老闆：這幅畫儿是明代的，現在世界上只有這一幅了。

學生：明代的？怎麽看起來這麽新呢？

老闆：噢！我們重新(1)整理過，比原來的好多了。

學生：這幅畫兒多少錢呢？

老闆：現在明代的畫兒越來越少了，我們只有這一幅了……

學生：我知道這是古畫兒，到底(2)要多少錢呢？

老闆：我們對(3)外國朋友總是特別客氣……

學生：你到底要多少錢啊？

老闆：這幅畫兒要是(4)在別的店裏，要三千塊。我賣給你，只要一千塊就行了。

學生：一千塊？太貴了！

老闆：一千塊是我的成本，我連一塊錢都不賺。

學生：五百塊，行不行？

老闆：開玩笑！要是五百塊賣給你，那我就賠五百塊！

學生：我是個窮學生，根本買不起(5)一千塊錢的畫兒。再見再見！

老闆：來來來來來，別走別走！你覺得這幅太貴，我們有比較便宜的。你看這幅人物畫兒……

學生：我不喜歡人物畫兒。我就是(6)要這幅山水畫兒。要是不便宜一點兒，我只好(7)不買了。

老闆：別走別走！八百塊賣給你了！

學生：太貴了！太貴了！我還有事兒，我得走了！

老闆：七百塊怎麼樣？

學生：我只有五百塊錢，多一塊都買不起！

老闆：好吧好吧！五百塊錢，賣給你了！

（二）在宿舍裏

學生：我今天逛古董市場，買了一幅山水畫兒，便宜極了。那個老闆本來要一千塊錢，後來五百塊就賣給我了。

同屋：真巧，我今天也在古董市場買了一幅畫儿。

學生：給我看看！

同屋：我最喜歡山水畫儿。你看這幅，真棒！

學生：哎呀！怎麼跟我買的一模一樣？你花了多少錢？

同屋：我才(8)花了一百塊！

學生：糟糕！又(9)上當(10)了！

∽ 语法点（yǔfǎdiǎn）

(1) 这幅画儿我们**重新**整理过。
   We have tidied up this painting.

   重新, meaning "again" or "once more," usually modifies disyllabic or polysyllabic words or phrases. If it is used to modify a monosyllabic verb, the verb must be followed by a complement. 再 or 又 may precede it.

   1. 请你再重新讲一次。
      Please explain it again.

   2. 他又重新写了一次，可是还是不太好看。
      He wrote it a second time, but it still didn't look good.

   Sometimes 重新 doesn't indicate a simple identical repetition, but indicates doing something in a different way so as to do it more satisfactorily than the first time.

   3. 原来的文章太长了，他又重新写了一篇，只有五百个字。
      The article he wrote the first time was too long. He wrote a second one which had only 500 characters.

   4. 这个办法不好，你最好再重新想个办法。
      This solution is not good. You'd better think of some other way.

(2) 我知道这是古画儿，**到底**要多少钱呢？
   I know that this is an ancient painting. How much does it really cost?

   到底 is often used in an interrogative sentence to indicate an attempt to get a definitive answer. It may precede the subject. In English the equivalent is usually expressed by intonation. Don't use 到底 when answering a question with 到底.

1. A: 你到底哪天去呢？还是快点儿决定吧！

   A: When exactly will you go? You'd better decide as soon as possible.

   B: 我已经决定下星期一去了。

   B: I've decided to go there next Monday.

2. 这幅画到底是在附近的古董店买的还是在王府井买的？

   Where exactly did you buy this painting? Was it at the antique store nearby or in Wangfujing?

(3) 我们对外国朋友总是特别客气。

We are especially polite to foreign friends.

对 in this context means "treat." 对 modifies a descriptive word or phrase showing somebody's attitude towards the person or thing represented by the object of 对. 对 must occur after the subject. The word or phrase modified can be either positive or negative.

1. 学校对外国学生太好了！宿舍里不但有空调，还有电视和电话呢！

   The school treats foreign students too well! The dorms not only have air conditioning, but also a color TV and a telephone.

2. 这家银行的职员对人不太客气。

   The clerks in this bank are not very polite to people.

3. 他对你怎么样？

   How does he treat you?

(4) 这幅画儿要是在别的店里，要三千块。

This painting would cost three thousand dollars in another store.

要是 is mostly used in conjunction with 就 in the second clause. 就 can be omitted, especially when there is another adverb or auxiliary word such as 会, 可以, 只好, 简直, etc., or a question word in the second clause.

1. 你现在住在中国，要是还坚持原来的生活习惯，（就）会觉得很不方便。

   You are now living in China. If you still hold on to your old habits of living, you will find things very inconvenient.

2. 你要是不习惯用筷子，可以用刀叉。

   If you are not accustomed to using chopsticks, you may use a knife and fork.

3. 要是你觉得很不舒服，为什么不请一天假，休息休息呢？

   If you are not feeling well, why don't you ask for one day off to rest?

(5) 我是个穷学生，根本买**不起**一千块钱的画儿。

I am a poor student; I simply cannot afford to buy a painting for one thousand dollars.

买不起 means "cannot afford to buy." Other verbs can be used and mean "cannot afford *V-ing*," e.g. 住不起那么贵的旅馆, 上不起大学, 坐不起飞机.

(6) 我**就是**要这幅山水画儿。

It is this landscape painting that I want.

This 就是 is the same as the one in L. 7, Note (1). It is used to express a determined attitude. Also see L. 8, Note (1).

1. 我说了半天，他就是不信。

   I spent quite a while trying to convince him, but he simply wouldn't believe me.

2. 我说不行就是不行！你不要再问了！

   When I say no, it means "no." Don't ask again!

(7) 要是不便宜一点，我**只好**不买了。

If you can't make it cheaper, I'll have no choice but to not buy it.

只好 is an adverb and indicates that one has to do something because he/she can't avoid the situation.

1. 学校附近没有邮局，我只好到城里去。

   There is no post office close to the school. I'll have to go downtown.

2. 她病了，只好请一天假，在宿舍里休息。

   She was sick, so she had no choice but to take the day off and stay in the dormitory.

(8) 我**才**花了一百块！

I only spent a hundred dollars!

才 is used before a number –*AN* phrase to indicate that the number is small, with 才 pronounced in the neutral tone and the numeral stressed. It applies only to a completed event.

1. 这幅画儿才卖两百块钱，真便宜！

This painting costs only two hundred dollars; it's really cheap!

2. 我才用了半个钟头就把功课写完了。

I finished my homework in only half an hour.

(9) 糟糕！**又上当了！**

Oh no! I've been conned again!

又 indicates repetition of an action or state and only applies to past or inevitable events. 又 is different from 再 in that 再 indicates a repetition which has not yet been realized or is to be realized.

1. 昨天我又到银行去换了五百块美元。

I went to the bank again yesterday to exchange five hundred U.S. dollars.

2. 明天又是星期天了，你打算做什么呢？

It's going to be Sunday again tomorrow. What do you plan to do?

3. 你已经上了他两次当了。下次小心一点儿，别再上当了。

You have already been taken in by him twice. You'd better be careful not to be fooled again.

(10) 又上当了！

上当 is in the passive voice. 我上当了 means "I was conned." There is no active voice for this word. "I was cheated by him" is 我上了他的当.

✎ 练习 (liànxí)

I. Answer the following questions using the structures provided.

1. 你买东西的时候会不会讲价？为什么？（只要…就行了）

2. 你喜欢不喜欢坐出租汽车？为什么？（上当）

3. 中国人习惯晚上洗澡，你可以也改成晚上洗澡吗？（就是…）

4. 很多人喜欢逛古董市场，因为东西很便宜，你呢？你喜欢逛古董市场吗？（本来…，后来…，现在…）

5. 你到中国来很长时间了吗？中国话说得怎么样？（才）

6. 你觉得这两件衣服有没有什么不同？（A跟B一模一样）

7. 你觉得自己是个穷学生还是个有钱的学生？你上大学的时候要不要工作？为什么？（只好）

II. Rearrange the phrases in the parentheses to make a logical sentence.

1. 我是个穷学生，（这么，呢，贵，住，宿舍，怎么，得起，的）？

2. （山水画儿，整理，我们，把，重新，这幅，过），所以看起来跟新的一模一样。

3. （的玩笑，总是，这个老板，开，外国学生，喜欢），对我们不太客气。

III. Fill in the blanks with only one character.

> 要，本，来，起，幅，么
> 就，新，到，少，多，对

A: 这 _____ 山水画儿看起 _____ 贵得很，我怕我根 _____ 买不 _____ 。

B: 一点儿都不贵，本来是九百块钱，现在只 _____ 五百块钱，我们 _____ 学生总是特别客气的。

A: 太贵了，你重 _____ 说个价吧！

B: 五百块钱怎 _____ 会太贵呢？好吧好吧，你说你 _____ 底想出（to bid）多 _____ 钱呢？

A: 一百块吧！

B: _____ 给五十块吧！一百五十块卖给你了！一块钱也不能少，再少我 _____ 得赔钱了！

A: 行，就一百五十块吧！

IV. Complete the dialogues or sentences using *v.* 得起 **or** *V.*不起。

1. 那家饭馆的饭菜太贵了，我根本 _____ 。

2. 看电影（diànyǐng, movie）很便宜，只要5块钱，谁都 _____ 。

3. 住在首都得花很多钱，我 _____ 。

4. 虽然现在私家车比以前便宜了一些，开的人也多了，但是我是个穷学生，_____ 私家车。

5. 上大学是很贵的，所以有些穷人的孩子 _____ 大学。

V. Complete the dialogues or sentences with the expressions provided.

1. A: 你不是想买幅人物画儿吗？怎么买了幅山水画儿回来了？

   B: _____ 。（本来…，后来…，所以…）

2. 银行职员：先生，您单子填错了，请 _____ 。（重新）

   学生：好吧好吧！请你再给我一张单子。

3. A: 对不起，我们没有单人间了，双人间行不行？

   B: 不行，_____ 。（就是[simply]）

VI. Translate into Chinese.

1. Have you actually seen a Ming landscape painting (use 到底)? This painting is not at all a restored ancient painting! It (它, tā) looks just the same as the one I saw in another antique store, and that painting was only 200 dollars. (use 才)

2. You faked your signature (签错) again. I don't want to be fooled by you anymore. If you won't rewrite a check for me, I would rather take cash.

3. I just don't believe that you sold this figure painting to me at a loss. Stop joking! You simply cannot afford to lose 500 dollars.

VII. Composition

Shopping in China can be a very interesting experience. Not only can one polish one's Chinese, one can also learn how to deal with street peddlers. Imagine you are writing a guide book for tourists. What are some good methods for haggling with or avoiding peddlers? What can you learn from your shopping experiences as a foreigner in China?